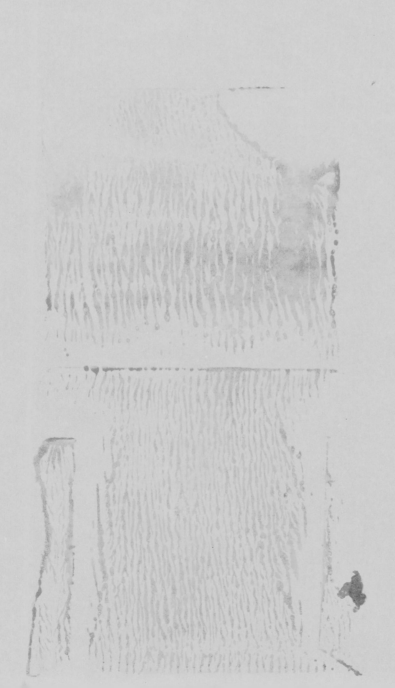

Great
CANDLES

ACKNOWLEDGEMENTS

To Mariarita Macchiavelli, without whose energy, help, and inspiration this book would never have been written.

Particularly warm thanks:

To my son Fienn, whom I neglected in order to make candles and write this book.

To Giuditta Pellizzoni and Clizia Ornato, for their help with the instructional photos.

To Muriel Rolland of Point à la Ligne, for her encouragement and generosity in creating such splendid images.

To the Graziani Wax Factory of Livorno, for the use of their materials and for their friendly advice.

To David Constable, candle maker, who has inspired me in this crafts for 20 years.

To the executive staff of Idee per Creare, for their encouragement.

To Cristina Sperandeo and the Manuali Fabbri editorial staff, for their patience and understanding, especially with my poor Italian language skills.

And a special thanks to Alberto and Matteo, for their beautiful and warm photos.

Editor: Cristina Sperandeo
Graphic design and layout: Paola Maserra and Amelia Verga with Milena Miron
Translation: Chiara Tarsia

Library of Congress Cataloging-in-Publication Data Available

10 9 8 7 6 5 4 3 2 1

Published by Sterling Publishing Company, Inc.
387 Park Avenue South, New York, N.Y. 10016
Originally published in Italy and © 1997 by R.C.S. Libri & Grandi Opere S.p.A., Milan
under the title *Candele*
English translation © 1999 by Sterling Publishing
Distributed in Canada by Sterling Publishing
C/o Canadian Manda Group, One Atlantic Avenue, Suite 105
Toronto, Ontario, Canada M6K 3E7
Distributed in Great Britain and Europe by Cassell PLC
Wellington House, 125 Strand, London WC2R 0BB, England
Distributed in Australia by Capricorn Link (Australia) Pty Ltd.
P.O. Box 6651, Baulkham Hills, Business Centre, NSW 2153, Australia

Sterling ISBN 0-8069-5921-5

Great CANDLES

Stewart D'Arcy Hyder

Sterling Publishing Co., Inc.
New York

Table of contents

Foreword

Mankind has always been fascinated by fire, and it's possible that our earliest gods lived in the depths of volcanoes. Even today many of our oldest surviving cultures revere the volcano's fire as the goddess Pele. All of Earth is considered Pele's creation and every stone her child. Her gift to mankind is a strand of her hair, a single small flame. Indeed, the ability to hold the hair of Pele – to tame the flame – is possibly our most important achievement, because being able to create and use fire is what makes humans unique among animals, and it is from this ability that every other facet of civilization has evolved.

The flickering light of a flame is truly magical. Despite the wonders of modern technology, we still light candles when we want to create a special mood or ambience. Whether the setting is for a romantic meal, a child's birthday celebration, a Christmas gathering, or a dinner party or just to create a relaxing atmosphere at the end of the day, we invariably choose candles.

Candles of different colors, of different sizes, of different shapes, of different textures. Candles indoors, candles outdoors. Candles lit, candles unlit. Candles for functionality, candles for decor.

A candle's mesmerizing flame stirs us today as fire has done since the dawn of time when our ancestors first held Pele's gift. The soothing hypnotic effect of candlelight is recognized in all societies and cultures, and it is used universally in religious institutions and ceremonies. The ambient effect of candlelight can evoke an emotional response that is immediate. Yet, it also throws us back in time to the primitive emotions of our earliest ancestors, those who gazed in awe at the volcano, revered it as a god, and brought the gift of its flame into our lives.

History

Before electricity became an energy source available to almost everyone, fire and candles were the only sources of artificial light. Now, although no longer a necessity, candles are still found in most homes, not merely for their decorative value, but because there is something very special about candlelight. Lighting a few candles immediately changes the ambience of a room, their warm flickering flames entrancing all who enter.

From the earliest times tapers, candles, and lamps were made by dipping rushes and cord in tallow. Tallow is an animal fat that produces acrid clouds of black smoke and an offensive smell when burned. Better quality candles made of beeswax were also made, but they were very expensive and only affordable by the church and the aristocracy. It was not until the early 19th century that industrialization and oil refining techniques led to the development of cheaper, longer burning, odor-free candles. Stearin (a chemical compound originally produced for the soap industry) and paraffin wax (a by-product of hydrocarbon oil refining) eventually changed the techniques of candle making and the lives of everyone.

Modern candles burn with a steady flame and usually do not drip unless there is a draft. If you happen to get spills of wax on clothing, furniture, or fabrics, allow the wax to cool and harden before you attempt to remove it. Scrape off as much of the hard wax as possible with a knife, then iron the affected area through a sheet of absorbent paper.

Finally, remember that your magical candle flame is also a potential fire hazard.

CANDLES

The crafts of the candle maker have changed considerably since the time when candles were the only means of lighting a home. The candle has changed from being purely utilitarian and functional to an object of art, design, and beauty. Today it is possible to make candles in so many colors, shapes, sizes, and designs that it is almost impossible to imagine a decor that would not be enhanced by the addition of a candle. Welcome to the world of the candle maker.

Materials

Candle making is very similar to cooking. With a few basic materials, it is possible to make a wide range of different creations and, like cooking, it is what you do with your materials and how you heat them that produces the end result in candle making. To make a candle you need wax and a wick. Both are available from crafts shops and specialty stores. It is also possible to buy candle making kits that contain all the materials you need to make a few simple candles. A kit can be a good introduction to candle making.

The most important material in candle making is the wax. For the projects in this book, no specific quantities of wax are given, because the amount for each candle will vary according to the size of the candle you want to make. To determine the amount you need for a specific mold, fill the mold with water, then pour the water into a measuring cup to see how much the mold held. For every 16 oz. of water you will need 1 1/4 lbs. of cold wax. If you melt too much wax, don't worry. You can reuse any extra for your next project.

Paraffin wax

Paraffin wax is the type most commonly used in candle making. It is available in large slabs from industrial suppliers. For the home candle maker, it is most convenient to buy wax flakes or pellets. You can buy dyed and undyed paraffin wax in pure form or premixed with stearin. You would probably find a 11 lb. slab the most convenient size to work with.

Stearin

Stearin is an additive for paraffin wax. It increases the hardness of the wax and makes the candle burn more slowly and evenly without dripping. It also causes the hot wax to shrink as it cools, which is an enormous help when making molded candles, because it allows them to slide out of the molds easily. For the projects in this book you will use a purchased paraffin wax, stearin mixture or add 10 percent stearin to all pure paraffin wax unless otherwise directed.

Beeswax

Beeswax is a natural product available in 8 1/2" x 16 3/4" preformed sheets or in blocks from art stores, crafts shops, apiary suppliers, and antique restorers. Beeswax sheets are particularly good for making candles with children, because the only heat required is that of a hair dryer. Beeswax has a particularly pleasant smell when burned, and any leftovers can be added to paraffin wax.

Paraffin wax candles that contain even a small amount of beeswax burn more slowly than candles without it. Most modern church candles contain 25 percent added beeswax.

Wicks

Selecting the right size wick is essential. If the wick is too thin for the candle, the flame will be small and may drown in a pool of molten wax as the candle burns. If the wick is too thick in proportion, the candle will smoke, drip badly, and burn very quickly. Wicks are made of braided cotton in many different diameters. The smallest wicks are for a candle 3/8" in diameter and the largest for a candle 3 3/4" in diameter. The sizes in between correspond to diameter increments of 3/8".

Dyes

Wax dyes are usually sold in solid or powder form. The dyes are very intense, so only a little bit needs to be added to color the wax.

Crayons

Pure wax crayons can be used to color wax for candle making, but if the crayons contain any impurities at all, they will adversely affect the burning properties of the candle. The color of dyed, hot, molten wax is different from that of cold, set wax, so do a color test before you pour your candle. You can test the color of your wax by putting a few drops onto a sheet of freezer paper and allowing it to cool and set.

Mold sealer

Mold sealer is a puttylike substance used to secure the wick in the mold and to prevent molten wax from leaking out.

Wax glue

Wax glue is a soft substance used to hold pieces of wax together. It can also be used to secure candles in candleholders.

Scents

Paraffin wax is almost odorless when it burns, but you can add scents to your candles if you like. You can use special candle scents or experiment with essential oils. Natural oils such as citronella can also be used. You can use scents in two different ways: Either add a few drops directly to the molten wax, or soak the wick prior to priming it.

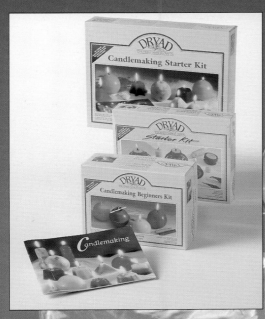

Equipment

Most of the equipment needed for candle making can be found around the house.

Double boiler

Ideally a double boiler for candle making should be made of stainless steel. If you don't have a double boiler, you can improvise by placing one pot on top of another, but the two-pot method may result in uneven heating of the wax, so you will need to be particularly careful about the temperature of the wax.

Dipping can

A dipping can is a tall, cylindrical metal container available in crafts shops and candle maker's supply stores. It is used for making dipped tapers and for overdipping candles. As a general guide, a dipping can measuring 12" x 24" (15 x 30 cm) will require about 6 1/2 lbs. (3 kg) of cold wax.

Thermometer

An accurate thermometer is an essential piece of equipment in candle making. The chemical structure of wax is different at different temperatures, so it is impossible to judge the temperature of liquid wax, which must be accurately measured. Wax thermometers are available in most crafts shops. A candy thermometer or any thermometer that registers 350°F and above is best.

Baking trays

A good assortment of baking trays and pans is invaluable in candle making. You will find many uses for them.

Freezer paper

Freezer paper has a special coating that does not absorb wax. It is ideal for covering work surfaces and for lining baking trays.

Wicking needles

Wicking needles are long steel needles used for inserting wicks into candles.

Skewers

Skewers are used for securing a wick to the base of a mold.

Crafts knife

You will find many uses in candle making for a crafts knife. You can cut a wick, trim the base of a candle, or cut beeswax sheets or stencils. Be sure you always work with a sharp blade, and cut away from your body to avoid injuring yourself.

Precautions and wisdom

Fire safety

Most candle making involves working with heat, and prolonged contact with molten wax can burn your skin. If hot wax spills on you, run very cold water over the affected area until the wax cools and hardens. Molten wax should be treated respectfully, the way you treat hot cooking oil. At temperatures below 221°F, wax will not catch fire, but as the temperature rises above this level, it becomes increasingly volatile. Never leave wax melting over heat unattended. If the wax does catch fire:

- Switch off the heat source immediately.
- Do not attempt to move the pan.
- Do not attempt to put out the fire with water; this will only spread it.
- Smother the flames with a damp cloth or a metal lid, then allow the pan to cool completely before touching it.

Before lighting any candle, be sure to secure it in a candleholder at a safe distance from any flammable material. If the candleholder itself is flammable, or if it is part of a decorative arrangement that contains flammable materials, extinguish the candles before they burn down to within a few inches of the holder. Never leave lit candles unattended.

Workshop wisdom

Candle making is not an inherently messy process, but accidents can happen. Always wear old clothes or an apron when you are making candles, and cover the floor with newspaper. Organize your workspace so that you have enough room to work. All tools and materials should be conveniently located. Never pour liquid wax into drains or sinks; it will immediately solidify and cause a blockage. If you have a small amount of wax left over after a project, pour it into a baking pan lined with freezer paper and save it for another project.

Clean your equipment by washing it in a plastic bowl filled with hot water. The wax will melt and float to the surface. As the water cools, the wax will solidify and you can skim it off and throw it away.

White spirits or turpentine can be used to dissolve small amounts of cold wax. Always allow wax to cool and solidify before attempting to clean up spills this way.

Candle racks

A candle rack is an important piece of equipment for making dipped candles. To make a rack, all you need are a few common items and a little patience.

Using the crafts knife or saw, carve two notches in one narrow (top) edge of each long board, making sure there is at least 3/8" between pairs of notches. Measure down 1 1/4" from the center of the notched edge and drill a 3/8"-diameter hole completely through each board.

Glue the bottom of the notched boards to the narrow side edges of the remaining board, centered. Allow to dry.

When the rack seems steady, glue the two shorter dowels into the notches. Allow to dry.

Slide the remaining dowel through the two holes drilled into the notched boards. If the rack seems wobbly, secure the long dowel with glue. Allow to dry.

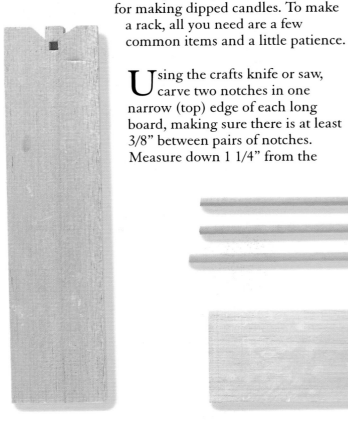

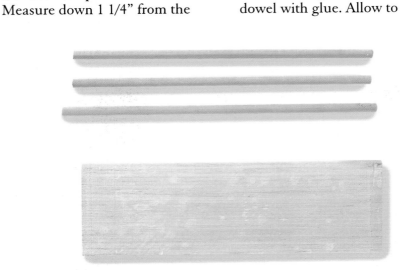

Priming the wicks

Materials and equipment

2 1/4 lbs. paraffin wax
Wicks
Large pot
Dipping can
Thermometer
Candle rack

Melting wax and priming the correct size wick are the two most essential skills in candle making. The heart of every good candle is a good wick; if the wick isn't just right, the candle will not burn correctly.

Put water into the large pot and the wax into the dipping can. Heat the wax gently until it melts and reaches 158°F, then turn off the heat.

Fold a length of wick in half and, holding it in the middle, immerse it in the molten wax for 60 seconds. Notice how air trapped in the wick is forced out and rises to the surface, while any moisture in the wick is forced out at the same time.

Remove the wick from the wax and gently pull it taut and straight between your thumb and forefinger.

Hang the wick over the candle rack to harden. Repeat this process with the remaining wicks.

DIPPED CANDLES

Hand-dipped candles, or tapers,
are simple to make and have an elegance
that mass-produced candles cannot match.

Simple tapers

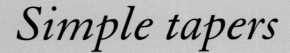

The candles are made in pairs by dipping the wick ends into a dipping can filled with molten wax. Layer upon layer of wax is built up on the wick with each successive dip, gradually building up the thickness of the candle. As the first dip sufficiently primes the wick, it is not necessary to use pre-primed wicks. You can dip into dyed or undyed wax.

A solid color candle is slightly translucent. You can also overdip a white candle in dyed wax. An overdipped candle has a more intense color than a solid color one.

Dipping cans hold a large amount of wax, so it makes sense to dip several pairs of candles at the same time. The exact amount of wax you will require depends on the size of your dipping can. As a general guide, 6 1/2 lbs. of cold wax is sufficient for a can that is 5" in diameter and 12" high.

To ensure success when making dipped candles, it is vital to use molten wax at the correct temperature. If the wax is too cool, the candle will have a lumpy appearance with white patches on the outside. If it is too hot, the previously formed layers will melt and you will have a well-primed wick but no candle!

With a little practice, you will be able to produce an even dip every time.

Step-by-step

Materials and equipment

Paraffin wax with stearin added

Wax dyes

3 wicks, 24" long

Dipping can

Large pot

Wooden spoon

Thermometer

Candle rack

Crafts knife

Skill level: Beginner

Fill the dipping can with cold wax. Place the dipping can into the pot and fill the pot with water to about halfway up the side of the can. Heat the water to melt the wax, stirring the wax occasionally. As soon as all the wax has melted, start checking its temperature with the thermometer. When the molten wax reaches 160°F, turn down the heat.

If your wax needs to be colored, add a small amount of dye and stir well. When fully mixed, test a few drops by placing them on a piece of freezer paper and letting them set. If you are not satisfied with the color, add a little more dye and repeat the process. Wax dyes are pretty intense, so add only a little bit at a time. Check the temperature of the molten wax to make sure it is 160 -163°F

Holding a piece of wicking in the middle, dip the free ends into the wax so that all but about 2" of

each end is immersed. Dip the wick ends in a smooth, steady motion; allow them to stay immersed for about 3 seconds, then carefully lift them out of the can.

Hang the wicks on the candle rack for about 3 minutes to dry, but do not let them touch each other.
While they dry, you can dip another pair of wicks, if you wish. Repeat the dipping and drying with all of your wicks until your tapers are the desired thickness.

To give the tapers a smooth, glazed finish, increase the temperature of the wax to 181°F for the final dip, dip them for 3 seconds, then hang them to cool. This process is called overdipping. When the tapers have cooled (about 50 minutes), trim the bases with the crafts knife to square them off. Another very quick overdip will give them a final polish. Hang the tapers until dry.

After the final overdip, the tapers must be cooled for at least an hour without handling. Hanging them on a candle rack allows the air to circulate freely around the tapers and keeps them from touching each other and possibly sticking together as they cool.

Rainbow tapers

These multicolored candles have an appeal that will brighten any contemporary setting.

Step-by-step

Skill level: Beginner

Make a couple of 10"-long white dipped tapers by immersing them several times in hot wax until they are the desired thickness. Use different colors of hot wax for successive dips, as directed below; be sure to allow tapers to dry between dips.

Add a small amount of yellow wax to the hot white wax and mix well, making sure the temperature never exceeds 163°F, then dip the tapers. Allow to dry. Dip the tapers into the hot wax again, stopping about 1 1/2" from the wick. Allow to dry. Add a little more yellow wax, mix, check the temperature, then dip the tapers again to 3" from the wick. Allow to dry.

Add a small amount of red wax to the hot yellow wax and mix well, making sure the temperature never exceeds 163°F, then dip the tapers to 3 1/2" from the wick. Allow to dry. Continue to alternate dipping and drying, immersing the tapers first to 5", then to 6 1/2", 8", and 9 1/2"

When you dip tapers into yellow and then red wax this way, the shading ranges from yellow to orange to red. To create tapers ranging from yellow to green to blue, dip them into yellow and then blue wax, paying particular attention to the central shading, which will be green.

Heat white wax to 185°F, then quickly dip the tapers for the last time to glaze them. Allow to dry. With the crafts knife, square off the bases. Hang the tapers on the candle rack; allow to dry.

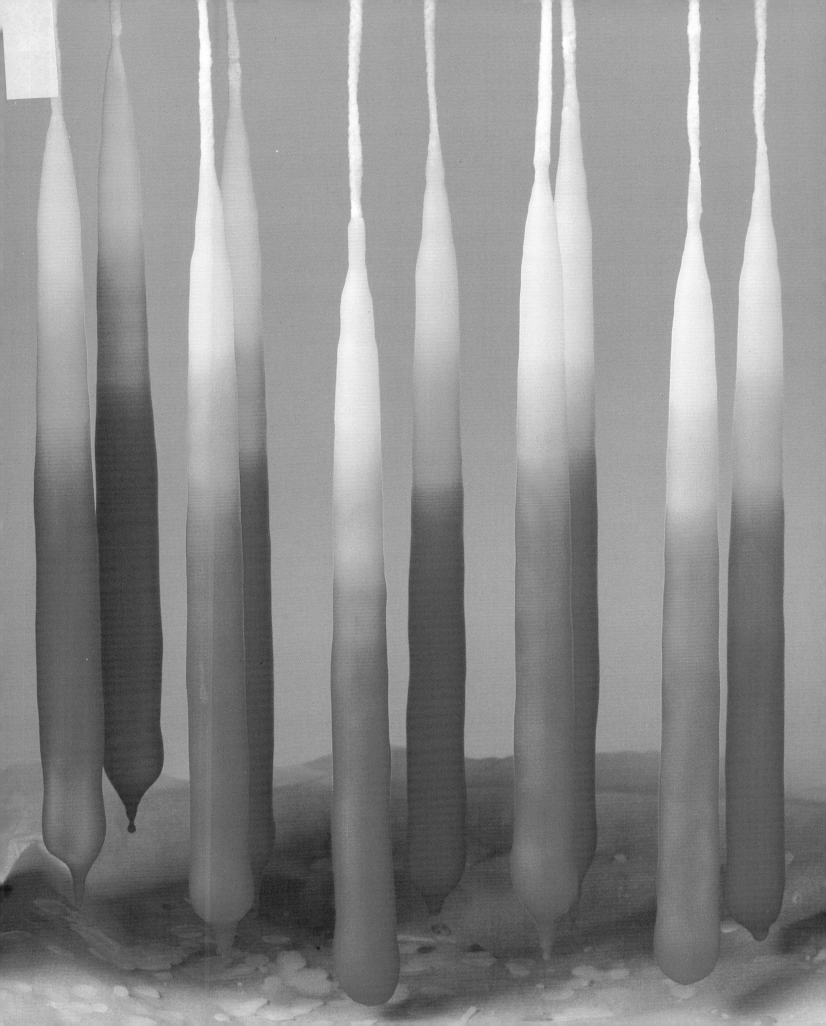

Twist candles

Materials and equipment
Two freshly dipped tapers, still warm and malleable
Rolling pin
Hair dryer
Crafts knife
Large pot
Dipping can

Skill level: Intermediate

The spiral twist is a classic candle shape suitable for all decors from traditional to contemporary. Twist candles look their best in simple holders. Purchased twists are frequently made in molds, but you can make them at home from hand-dipped tapers. You just flatten a warm taper with a rolling pin and then twist it by hand. As long as the taper is warm and malleable, the shaping is easy. You will find that a warm hair dryer can be a big help. Wax and water do not mix. If you use a rolling pin, soak it in hot water for 30 minutes beforehand, to prevent the wax from sticking as you roll it. If you don't have a rolling pin, you can use a glass bottle filled with warm water instead.

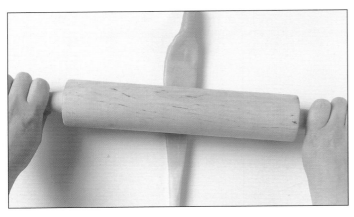

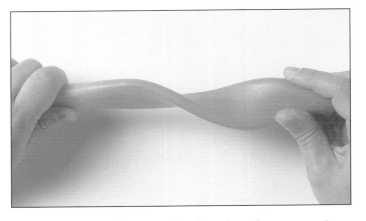

On a perfectly smooth, clean surface, roll and flatten the shaded center section of a warm taper to a thickness of about 1/4", leaving about 1" of the base unrolled. Use the hair dryer as necessary to keep the wax warm and pliable. If you use a simple one-color taper, leave about 2 1/4" untwisted at the tip.

Grasp the candle near the wick with the thumb and forefinger of one hand, then grasp the base in the same manner with your other hand, and start to twist the candle. Twist gently but steadily, keeping the wax pliable with the hair dryer. You will need to work quickly before the wax cools.

After twisting the candle, check that the base has not become distorted and that it will still fit into a candleholder. These candles are handmade, so unevenly spaced twists will merely add to their charm. Trim the base with a crafts knife, or reshape it with your fingers as necessary.

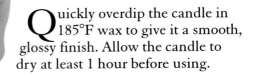

Quickly overdip the candle in 185°F wax to give it a smooth, glossy finish. Allow the candle to dry at least 1 hour before using.

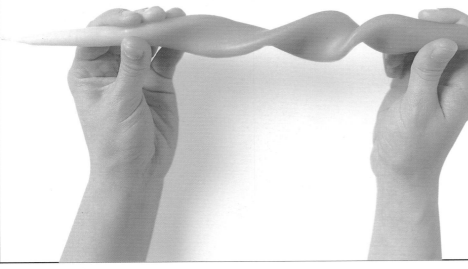

Snake candles

I call this the snake candle because it reminds me of a coiled cobra dancing to a snake charmer's flute.

The snake is a type of spiral candle, but it has a more casual feel than the twist. It is made in the same way as a normal hand-dipped taper, but after you have made the first few dips, when the base of the taper is about 3/8" in diameter and while the candle is still malleable, you coil it around a skewer. You then continue dipping in the normal way to build up the candle's thickness and finish it as you would for any ordinary taper.

When you display a homemade snake candle, people will wonder how you made such an unusual shape. Maybe you had a special spiral wick!

Pour wax and dye into the dipping can. Place the dipping can into the large pot; add water to the pot; then heat and melt the wax, stearin, and dye to 158°F. Keeping the temperature steady and checking the thermometer frequently, dip and redip the wick until the base of the taper is about 3/8" in diameter.

When the candle is the desired thickness, hang it to cool and dry, trim the base with the crafts knife, and overdip the candle in 185°F white wax for 1 second. Hang the candle to set completely for at least 1 hour before using.

Wipe the skewer with salad oil, which will act as a lubricant. While the taper is still warm and malleable, wind it around the skewer. Keep the taper workable by warming it with the hair dryer. After the taper is coiled, hang it on the candle rack to harden.

Continue to dip and redip the coiled candle until it is the desired thickness. The coil may loosen somewhat as the wax builds up and the weight increases.

Multi-wick tapers

Materials and equipment

Three freshly dipped rainbow tapers, still warm and malleable
Pencil
Freezer paper
Hair dryer
Crafts knife
Wax glue
Dipping can
Large pot
Thermometer

Skill level: Intermediate

Multiple candles stemming from a single base make an elegant and unusual focal point for both formal and informal dining.

These candles provide a lot of light, but they also generate a considerable amount of heat, especially if they have five or more wicks.

Use the pencil to draw a modified Z shape on freezer paper, making the angles about 90 degrees and gently curved, not sharp.

Use the hair dryer to warm a freshly dipped rainbow taper, gently bending the taper to match the Z pattern you drew.

Warm and bend 2 more tapers. Allow the bent candles to cool and harden about 20 minutes.

Using the crafts knife, diagonally cut away one side of each candle base to expose the wick.

Use the hair dryer to warm the bases of the candles until they are very soft and malleable. Press and mold the softened wax of the candle bases together to form one single base with the exposed wicks facing inward and the uncut sections facing outward. Fill any irregularities with wax glue and allow the base to harden.

Dip the newly formed base of the candle in wax heated to 158°F for 2 seconds. Repeat 3 times, allowing the candle to cool and harden between dips.

BEESWAX CANDLES

Beeswax has a delicious smell when it burns, which reputedly can enhance your health and well-being in addition to just smelling nice. The hexagonal honeycombing of beeswax sheets gives candles a natural-looking texture that works well with any contemporary or country decor.

Straight and tapered candles

Materials and equipment

Beeswax sheets, 8 1/2" x 16 3/4"
Primed wicks
Hair dryer
Metal ruler or straight edge
Crafts knife

Skill level: Beginner

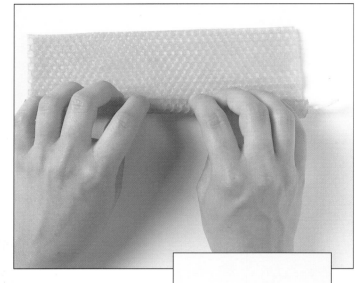

Straight-sided candle

Use the hair dryer to warm a rectangular sheet of beeswax so that it becomes pliable. Cut a primed wick about 3/4" longer than one short edge of the beeswax, then gently press the wick into the short edge.

Keeping the beeswax soft with the hair dryer, roll up the sheet around the wick, making sure that the wick is held firmly in place by the first roll and that the long top and bottom edges of the sheet remain fairly even.

When you have finished rolling up the sheet, press the free short edge into the side of the candle to secure it, smoothing it in place with your fingers.

Tapered candle

Use the metal straight edge and crafts knife to cut away a narrow triangle from one long edge of a beeswax sheet; save the triangle for another project.

Use the hair dryer to warm the beeswax so that it becomes pliable. Cut a primed wick about 3/4" longer than the second-shortest edge of the sheet, then gently press the wick into that edge.

Beginning at the wick edge, roll up the candle, keeping the base edges even, then secure and finish the free end as for the straight-sided candle.

You can make deeply spiraled candles (opposite) by cutting a beeswax sheet in half diagonally and rolling each half to make a candle. Secure and finish each free end along its entire length.

Flower candles

The flowers, the buzzing of bees, and the golden sweetness of honey are inextricably intertwined. For a summery feel at any time of year, nothing could be more appropriate than these pretty beeswax roses.

Use the smaller cookie cutter to cut out 3 hearts from a sheet of yellow beeswax and 5 hearts from a sheet of red beeswax. Use the large cookie cutter to cut out 4 hearts from the red beeswax and 4 hearts from a sheet of green beeswax.

Cut a small piece from the yellow beeswax sheet, roll it into a pea-size ball, flatten it, then wrap it around the center of the wick.

Using the hair dryer to keep the wax pliable, take a small yellow heart and wrap it around the ball and wick, pinching the base onto the wick. Add the remainder of the yellow hearts to form the center of the rose. Add the small red hearts and then the large red ones, working around the flower center to create the petals.

Add the large green hearts around the petals to form the leaves. Finish by trimming the wick at the base of the rose with the crafts knife.

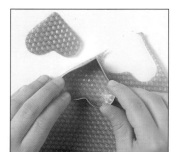

Bull's-eye candles and lanterns

Easy and quick to make, these candles are a good way to use up beeswax scraps from other projects. They also make perfect projects for beginners.

Bull's-eye candles

Materials and equipment
Scraps of beeswax sheets in assorted colors
Primed wick
Metal ruler
Crafts knife
Hair dryer
Skill level: Beginner

These candles are fun and easy for children to make in different colors. They also make great party favors. Using the ruler and crafts knife, cut out strips of different colored beeswax, making all the strips the same depth.

Soften the strips with the hair dryer and wrap them tightly around the wick to resemble sushi. Gently press each layer in place as you roll, to help the layers stick together. Secure and smooth the final free end in place.

For a bull's-eye that resembles a log, omit the wick at the center, roll and finish the candle as usual, then pierce the candle with a heated needle from the outside of the final layer all the way through to the other side and insert the wick.

Beeswax lanterns

Materials and equipment

2 sheets of beeswax,
8 1/2" x 16 3/4"
Primed wick, 4" long
Hair dryer
Crafts knife

Skill level: Beginner

Small and decorative, lantern candles can be used at each place setting for an informal dinner party.

Using more scraps

You can cut scraps of beeswax into small shapes such as triangles, squares, or circles, then pile them up to make the candlestick type of candle shown here. Pierce through the center of the candle from the top to the base with a heated wicking needle and insert the wick.

Press the wick against the shortest side edge of the larger sheet of wax. Using the hair dryer, soften the sheet and roll it tightly to make a straight-sided candle. While the candle is still warm, flatten the base and flare it slightly with your fingers until the candle stands on its own.

Use the crafts knife to cut 8 parallel and equidistant slits in the remaining wax sheet, stopping 3/8" from the long top and bottom edges.

Roll the slit sheet around the candle. Because the slits are longer than the candle, the strips between the slits will bend and bow outward. Shape them as you wish, pressing and smoothing the upper and lower edges of the lantern in place around the candle.

Sunflower candles

Making sunflower candles requires time, patience, and precision. But all of your hard work will pay off in the beautiful results you create.

Timing and temperature are very important in every step of making a sunflower candle. As you assemble all of the parts, make sure they stick together well. Using a hair dryer will keep the wax soft and pliable and prevent it from hardening before the flower parts are properly positioned and adhered.

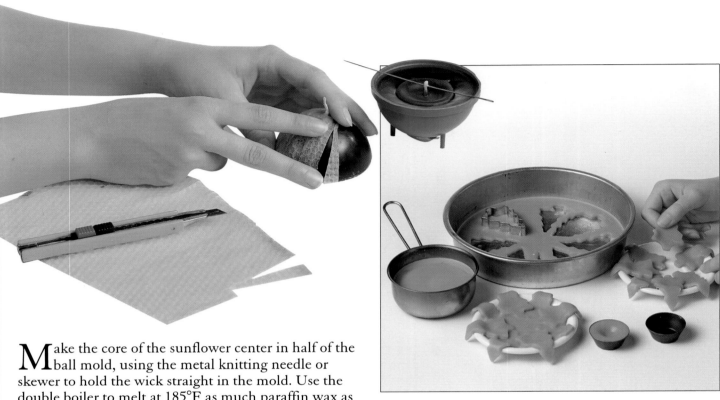

Make the core of the sunflower center in half of the ball mold, using the metal knitting needle or skewer to hold the wick straight in the mold. Use the double boiler to melt at 185°F as much paraffin wax as needed to fill the mold. Add brown dye to the hot wax and mix thoroughly with a wooden spoon. As the candle begins to cool, fill in with additional brown wax any indents that may have appeared on the flat surface. When the candle is completely cool and hard, take it out of the mold and cover the rounded surface with warmed triangular segments cut from the yellow beeswax sheet to complete the flower center.

Melt enough paraffin wax to make the leaves of the sepal, which will go underneath the petals of the sunflower and form its base. When the hot wax reaches 185°F, add green dye and mix well with a clean wooden spoon. Pour the hot green wax into the small round molds to a thickness of 1/8"; you will need 8 of these shapes. When the wax cools and solidifies enough to handle, release the round shapes from the molds. Flatten and arrange them to cover the saucer; make and add more wax shapes as needed. Pour the remaining hot green wax into a pie plate to a thickness of 1/8". Allow it to cool slightly as for the small molded shapes,

Materials and equipment
Paraffin wax with added stearin
Sheet of yellow beeswax
Wax dyes in brown, green,
yellow, and orange
Primed wick
Small plate or saucer
Mold, ball shape that separates
into halves
Molds, small round
Cookie cutter, Christmas tree
shape
Knitting needle or skewer
Thermometer
Wooden spoons
Hair dryer
Double boiler
Small sauce pots
Pie pans
Crafts knife
Slender spatula

Skill level: Advanced

Heat the petals with the hair dryer and arrange them in a pleasing and natural manner.

then use the cookie cutter to cut out 8 tree shapes that will be used as leaves. Arrange the leaves equidistantly around the saucer with the tips overhanging and covering the edges of the saucer; mold to the inner contours of the dish. Press firmly so that all wax parts stick to each other.

Melt more paraffin wax, this time adding yellow and orange dye to make a bright sunflower yellow. Use a clean wooden spoon to stir the hot wax until the temperature remains steady at 185°F. Pour the wax into a clean pie pan to a thickness of 1/8". When it has solidified but is still warm and malleable, cut out about 25 narrow, tapered petals. Curl the petals slightly and allow them to cool. Using the hair dryer and putty knife, quickly stick the yellow petals around the wax flower center. Allow to cool and harden.

You have now completed the two main sections of the sunflower. To stick them together, arrange the flower center and petals on top of the leaves, centered. Heat the putty knife and slide it between the upper and lower sections of the sunflower, heating them. When the wax begins to melt, carefully slide out the putty knife and press the upper and lower sections together. Allow to cool and harden.

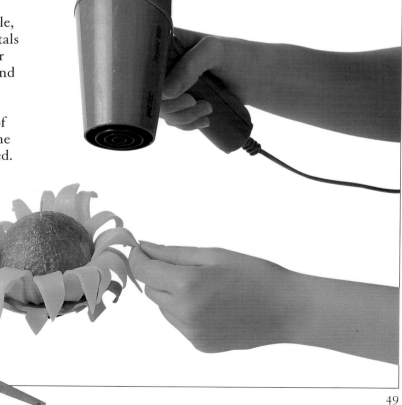

MOLDED CANDLES

Using molds offers a wide range of possibilities for the creative candle maker. Molds are easy to use and just about foolproof; a modest amount of skill can create professional-looking results. A simple 12-oz. drink can from soda or juice can be used to make perfect pillar candles.

Basic skills and techniques

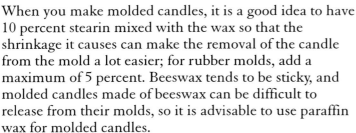

Molds can be purchased in a variety of shapes and sizes. They are usually made of rubber, plastic, metal, or glass. You can also turn common kitchen items into molds.

When you make molded candles, it is a good idea to have 10 percent stearin mixed with the wax so that the shrinkage it causes can make the removal of the candle from the mold a lot easier; for rubber molds, add a maximum of 5 percent. Beeswax tends to be sticky, and molded candles made of beeswax can be difficult to release from their molds, so it is advisable to use paraffin wax for molded candles.

A release agent acts as a barrier between the mold and the wax and can greatly aid the release of cooled candles, especially from intricate rubber molds. A good release agent that you probably have on hand is salad oil. When using rubber molds, it is best to add no more than 5 percent stearin to the wax, because the additive has a tendency to erode the rubber.

To determine the amount of cold wax you need for any mold, you can fill the mold with water, then empty the water into a measuring cup. For every 3 1/2 oz. of water you will need 3 oz. of wax. Molded candles require a primed wick that is at least 2" longer than the height of the candle. Always use plenty of mold sealer on the edges of the mold and wick.

Many purchased molds and drink cans have a flat base that gives them support and holds them upright; others without a flat base need to be supported. Rubber molds usually have a lipped edge that can be suspended through a strong cardboard collar to give them support and hold them in a vertical position. An alternative to suspension is setting the mold in a dry sand bath; you dampen the sand for cooling. Whenever possible, use a cold water bath to shorten the cooling time.

Candles can be cooled at room temperature, but that can take a surprisingly long time, especially if a candle is very large or thick. To speed up the process, you can cool candles in the refrigerator.

Pillar candles

All of the following projects use soda cans as molds, but you will notice that some of the step-by-step photos show a clear glass mold instead. I used the clear mold only so that you can see what actually happens inside the mold.

Although this section focuses on soda cans as molds, the basic molding and decorating techniques presented here are applicable to almost any kind of molded candle.

Plain pillar candles

The simple elegance of these molded pillar candles makes them appropriate for just about any occasion. Soda cans are ideal for making pillar candles.

Make a slit in the top of a soda can with a crafts or utility knife. Insert tin snips or sturdy scissors into the slit and carefully cut around the edge of the can to remove the top. Be careful not to dent or mar the sides of the can. As you cut the top, the can may distort a little, but it's nothing to worry about.

Make a hole in the center of the base of the can with an awl.

Any dents or distortions created by cutting off the top of the can be eliminated by placing the can on its side on a smooth surface, pressing a metal spoon inside the can over the dent, and rolling the can back and forth until smooth.

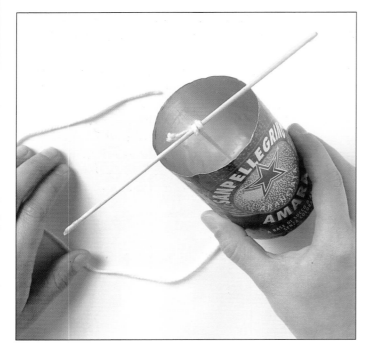

lace wax and stearin in the double boiler. Heat water in the bottom of the double boiler until the wax melts. Keep the temperature of the wax at 194°F. Add wax dye, stirring it into the molten wax a little at a time, until the desired shade is achieved.

When the molten wax is 194 -198°F, pour it carefully into the center of the mold, making sure it doesn't splash onto the sides of the mold. Fill the mold to within 3/8" of the top. Tap the sides of the mold gently to release any trapped air bubbles.

Thread a length of primed wick through the hole in the bottom of the mold. Tie the wick around the skewer to hold it at the top of the mold. Invert the mold, pull the top of the wick (the end poking through the hole) taut, and press a generous amount of mold sealer around it to secure it and seal the hole.

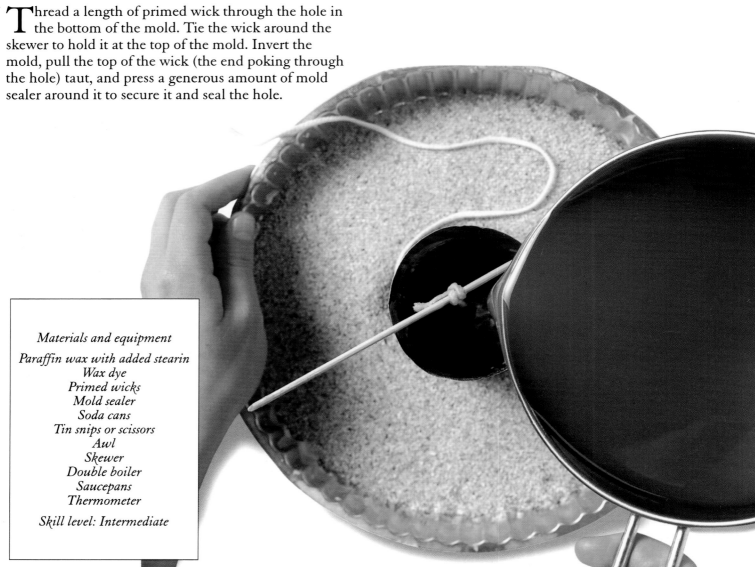

Materials and equipment

Paraffin wax with added stearin
Wax dye
Primed wicks
Mold sealer
Soda cans
Tin snips or scissors
Awl
Skewer
Double boiler
Saucepans
Thermometer

Skill level: Intermediate

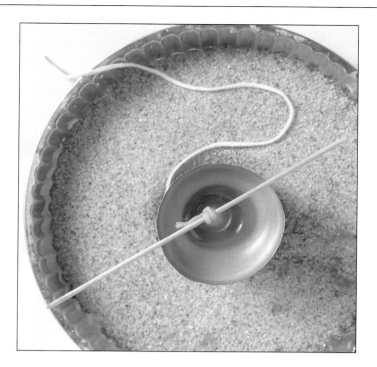

As the wax cools, an indentation will form around the wick. Fill it up with wax heated to 194 -198°F .

Let the wax cool until completely set. Remove the skewer and mold sealer, and the candle should slide right out of the mold. Trim the wick with scissors and stand the candle on a warm baking tray so that the base of the candle softens and becomes smooth and level. It should be unnecessary to overdip these candles; however, if there are any slight surface imperfections, they can be corrected by overdipping in molten wax at 198°F.

Reserve any leftover wax for a different project.

Place the filled mold into the saucepan, then place a heavy object (such as a book or paperweight) on top of the mold so that it will not float after water is added. Fill the saucepan with cold water to within 3/4" of the top of the mold, being careful not to splash any water into the wax. Allow the wax to cool. If you prefer, you can place the mold in the refrigerator to cool.

Striped pillar candles

These brightly colored and striped pillar candles bring a cheerful look to any decor. They are made using the same techniques as plain pillar candles. They are a great way to use up variously colored wax bits left over from other candle making projects.

Horizontally striped candles

Prepare the mold and wick.

Put different colors of wax into individual saucepans and heat until the wax melts and the temperature holds at 194 - 198°F.

Pour one color of melted wax into the mold to the desired depth. Allow to cool. Pour in another color of melted wax and allow it to cool. Continue adding and cooling layers of colored wax until the mold is filled. Be sure to check the temperature before each pouring.

Finish the striped pillar candles in the same manner as for the plain pillars.

Diagonally striped candles

This candle is a simple variation of the horizontally striped candle and is made in almost exactly the same way.

To create stripes on the diagonal, support the mold in sand at an angle somewhat off the vertical. Pour and cool the wax layers in the same manner as for the horizontally striped pillar candle.

When the wax nears the top of the mold, remove the mold from the sand and set it upright on a sturdy surface, then pour in the last layer and finish the candle as usual.

Chunk candles

Chunk candles can be made in any rigid mold. The larger the outer surfaces of the mold, the more the chunks will be visible.

Wax chunks are made in the following way: Pour different colors of wax into individual ice cube trays to a depth of about 3/4". Allow the wax to harden. After it has thoroughly cooled and hardened, release the slabs of wax from the trays and cut them into 3/4" cubes with the crafts knife. You can also use wax leftovers from other projects or purchased chunks. It isn't necessary for all of the chunks to be exactly the same size.

Prepare the mold and wick as usual. Loosely fill the mold with wax chunks.

Heat clear wax in the double boiler to a temperature of 194 - 198°F. Keep the wax at this temperature, frequently checking the thermometer.

Pour the melted wax into the mold to completely cover the solid chunks, stopping about 3/8" below the top of the mold. Tap the sides of the mold to release any trapped air bubbles.

Materials and equipment
Clear paraffin wax (no stearin)
Colored wax chunks
Primed wick
Mold sealer
Ice cube trays
Soda-can mold
Skewer
Double boiler
Thermometer
Crafts knife

Skill level: Intermediate

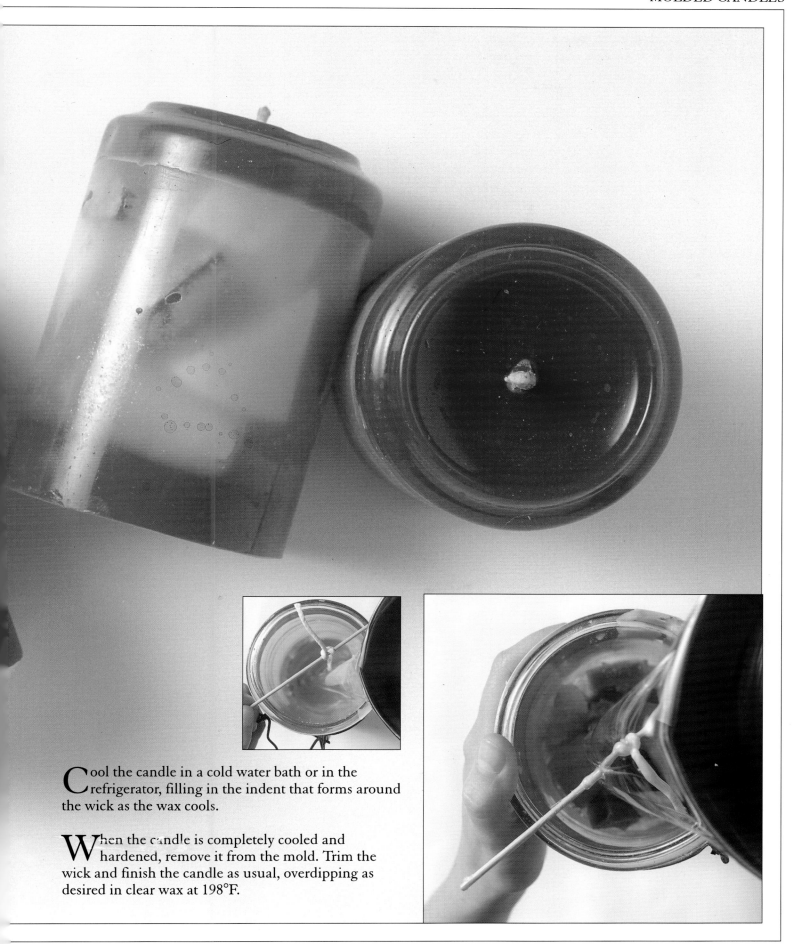

Cool the candle in a cold water bath or in the refrigerator, filling in the indent that forms around the wick as the wax cools.

When the candle is completely cooled and hardened, remove it from the mold. Trim the wick and finish the candle as usual, overdipping as desired in clear wax at 198°F.

Ice-sculpted candles

Skill level: Intermediate

Ice-sculpted candles honeycombed with cavities and tunnels make attractive and interesting conversation pieces on any table. These candles are made in a manner similar to that of the chunk candles. The main differences are that you use a core candle instead of a regular primed wick and ice cubes instead of wax ones. Also, instead of supporting the wick with a skewer, you use a wicking needle.

To make a core candle, cut a piece of wick as long as the height of your drink can plus 2". Repeatedly dip and cool the wick in 158°F melted wax to make a hand-dipped taper about 5" in diameter. If you prefer, you can use an ordinary household candle that has been cut to the proper length instead of making a taper.

Wick up the mold, using a core candle instead of a regular primed wick: Insert the core candle, wick first, into the mold and thread the wick through the hole in the base of the mold; secure the wick with mold sealer. Heat the metal pin and push it through the base of the core candle to secure it in a central position at the base of the mold.

Heat wax in the double boiler to 176°F. Pour wax into the mold to a depth of 3/8" and allow to cool.

Fill the mold with broken ice cubes.

Pour 176°F wax over the ice cubes to completely cover them, then put the mold in the refrigerator to cool and harden the candle. As the candle cools, check it frequently and top up the indent that forms with more melted wax.

When the candle has completely set, remove it from the mold. Work over the sink or a bowl, because the ice will have melted and the mold will contain water.

Granite and marble candles

Marble candles

Making a marbled candle is very similar to making a plain pillar candle. The veining of the marbled effect is created by dribbling a small amount of a contrasting color wax down the sides of the mold and allowing it to set before pouring in the main candle color.

These candles should be quickly overdipped in wax at 203°F to give a highly polished finish.

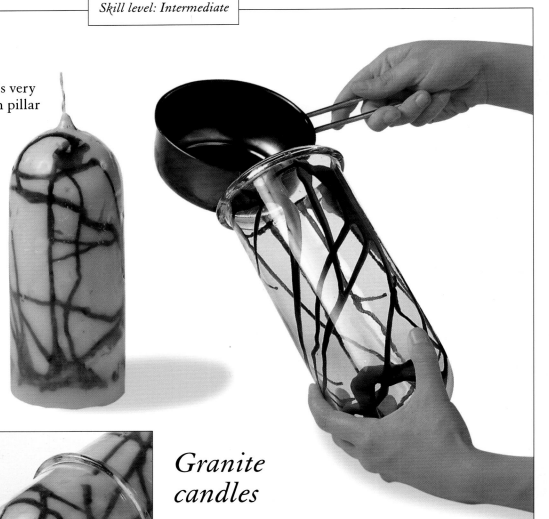

Granite candles

These granite candles look as though they have been freshly cut from solid rock.

Making a granite candle is almost identical to making a chunk candle. The only real difference is that the chunks for a granite candle are broken into small fragments instead of being cut into cubes. The wax poured over the fragments should be at the relatively low temperature of 158°F.

Don't smooth out the surface of the candle after it is released from the mold. The rough, pitted surface will enhance its natural look.

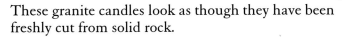

Candles made in rubber molds

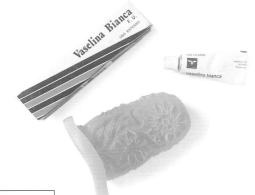

Skill level: Intermediate

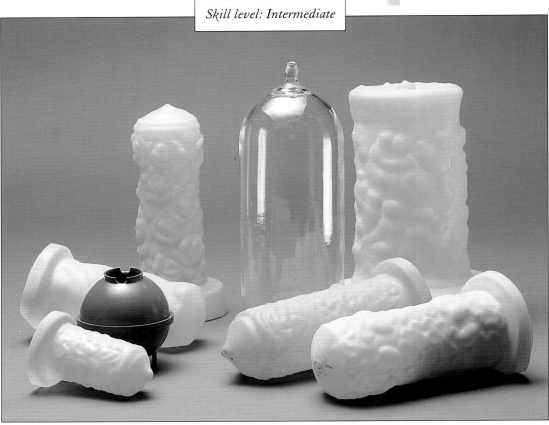

Rubber molds are available in a wide variety of shapes. They offer the candle maker an opportunity to create candles with intricately textured and embossed surfaces, which are particularly attractive when given an antique finish.

Making a candle in a rubber mold is very similar to making a pillar candle. The deeply embossed surface of a rubber mold can hamper the release of a cooled candle, however, so it is best to always coat the inside surfaces of the mold with a release agent, such as salad oil or petroleum jelly, before filling the mold with wax.

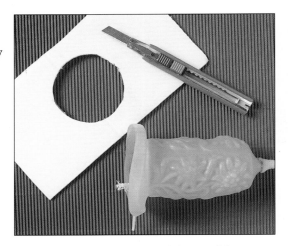

Because of their flexibility, rubber molds need support. The open end of the mold usually has a wide, flat lip that can be slipped over a stiff cardboard collar.

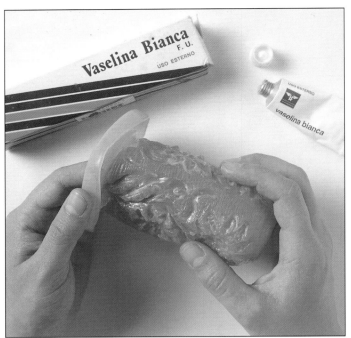

After wicking up the mold, fit the cardboard collar under the lip of the mold, suspend the mold by placing it into a suitable container so that the collar is supported on the open top end of the container and the sides and bottom of the mold don't touch the inside surfaces of the container.

Drinking glasses, jars, or even coffee cans make good containers, because they can be partially filled with cold water that will not only support the candle but also act as a water bath to help cool the wax. The wider the lip of your container, the wider the cardboard collar will have to be, so if you need to make a new collar, do it after you select the container.

Fill the mold with hot wax, gently tap the sides of the mold to release any air bubbles that may be trapped in the embossing, and top off any indents that form around the wick.

A llow the candle to cool completely, then remove the mold carefully from the candle to avoid marring its embossed surface.

T o accentuate the embossed surface of the candle, an antique finish can be applied. First, the raised part of the embossing is carefully covered with petroleum jelly, which will act as a barrier to the paint that will be applied. The entire surface of the candle is then painted, making very sure that the paint penetrates to the deepest nooks and crannies of the embossing. Finally, the candle is then wiped and polished with a cloth, which removes the paint from the raised areas while leaving it in the recesses.

Candles made in plastic molds

Plastic molds have hard, smooth sides. The molds are available in a wide range of shapes and sizes. Many are manufactured with supports incorporated into them. Some are made in two parts that are easily separated to release the finished candle. The ball mold is an example of a two-part plastic mold. All of the techniques described for making candles in drink cans can be applied to candles made in plastic molds.

Ball candles

The materials and equipment used for making a ball candle are basically the same as for a plain pillar candle. The techniques are also the same. Always cover your work surface with freezer paper so that cleanups of any spills will be easier.

Two-part molds, such as ball molds, will generally leave a visible seam on the finished candle. The seam can be removed by carefully paring it away with a sharp crafts knife. The trimmed candle can then be overdipped as necessary or as desired.

CONTAINER CANDLES

An alternative to making candles in molds is making them in decorative containers that become a permanent housing. The container provides the decoration and also functions as a candleholder. The wax and wick of a container candle serve one simple purpose: to provide light.

Step-by-step

These tin cans, which might have been thrown away when their contents were used up, have found new life as candle containers. The addition of citronella oil to the wax makes them ideal for outdoor use. Remember that when the wax melts, it will heat the metal of the can, so avoid touching it when it's hot and don't put it on surfaces that might be damaged by heat.

Making candles in containers, whether they are tin cans or terra-cotta pots, is very easy.

Secure a primed wick in the base of your container with a little mold sealer, and pour a little wax heated to 185°F in the double boiler into the container. Allow the wax to set.

When the wax has set, pour in a little more hot wax and allow it to set, checking that the wick remains upright. Repeat until the container is filled to within 3/8" of the top. Top off any well that develops in the final layer and trim the wick as necessary.

Candles in terra-cotta pots

Terra-cotta has a timeless appeal and makes an ideal container for candles. The natural simplicity of terra-cotta will compliment any country or outdoor setting and is equally at home with many contemporary decorative themes.

Many terra-cotta garden pots have a hole in the bottom, which can be easily sealed by putting a small piece of plastic wrap, or even a coin, over the hole and pouring about 1/2" of sand on top of it. The first layer of wax will seal the base of the candle.

Sand candles

Beautiful candles can be made with even simple materials, and a sand candle is one of the most striking and beautiful candles you can make. As the candle burns the light radiates through the sand.

A sand candle is the only type of candle for which it is recommended to heat the wax directly over a heat source because the wax has to be brought to a higher temperature than the boiling point of water, which is the maximum temperature possible using a double boiler. The wax has to be heated slowly and the temperature constantly monitored. Such a high temperature is necessary so that the heat of the wax can heat and evaporate the moisture in the sand, which is present at the minimum level needed for the sand to hold its shape.

Put the damp sand into a container larger than the size of the candle you want to make. Press the sand down firmly. Press the small bowl into the moist sand. If any sand is displaced around the edges of the bowl, press it firmly back in place around the edges of the bowl. Carefully remove the bowl, being careful to not disturb the sand.

Heat dyed wax gently over a direct heat source, constantly monitoring the temperature. As soon

as it reaches 248°F, slowly and carefully pour the wax into the indentation in the sand. After a few minutes the hot wax will displace the moisture in the sand. Some wax will seep into the sand. Top off the indentations formed by the seepage as necessary.

As the wax cools and hardens, a well will form in the center. Using the wicking needle, poke a hole down through the center of the well and insert the primed wick. Support the wick with the skewer. Top off the well as needed with wax heated to 203°F.

Allow the candle to completely cool, then remove it from the sand and brush away any loose sand. Cut and trim the wick as necessary.

Materials and equipment

Dyed paraffin wax mixed with
added stearin
Primed wick
Large pan (with lid) for
melting wax
Thermometer
Large container
Damp sand
Small bowl
Wicking needle
Skewer
Crafts knife

Skill level: Intermediate

Fire safety

At the temperatures required to make this candle, the wax can become volatile. Pay particular attention to the fire hazard warning on page 16, and make sure you have the lid to the pan nearby in the unfortunate event that you may need it. Pay careful attention to the temperature.

Floating candles

Materials and equipment
Dyed paraffin wax with added stearin
Primed wick
Double boiler
Thermometer
Small metal molds
Wicking needle
Crafts knife

Skill level: Beginner

All candles float, and these pretty little candles take advantage of that fact. A glass bowl full of water with one or more candles floating in it makes a stylish alternative to a conventional candlestick. Metal petit four molds with their fluted edges are ideal for making floating candles. But you can use any small smooth-sided metal container whose top opening is wider than its base. It is important that the top of a floating candle is at least as wide as its base (preferably wider) to add stability to the candle as it floats.

Heat dyed wax in the double boiler to a temperature of 194°F, checking the temperature with the thermometer. Fill the petit four molds with wax. Allow the wax to cool and harden.

When the wax is set, the candles will slip out easily from their molds; notice how the fluting shows daintily on the outside of the candles. Heat the wicking needle and press it

down through the center of each candle, which will make a hole and melt the wax around the hole. Immediately push a wick through the hole formed by the needle. The molten wax around the hole will set and seal the hole around the wick.

Trim the wick at the top and bottom of the candle. Remember that for floating candles, unlike other molded candles, the wider end of the candle is the top.

Chocolate candles

Delightful chocolate candles make a surprise after-dinner offering to amaze and delight your guests. These little candles are made in almost the same way as floating candles, using small petit four and candy molds.

Skill level: Beginner

Make chocolate candles in the same manner as for floating candles, using wax dyed chocolate brown. The brown color can be obtained by using a brown crayon or by mixing red and green wax dyes together.

Make the dye a rich brown. Test a little on freezer paper before pouring the candles. Remember when inserting the wick that the larger end of the candle is the top.

Ice cream candles

Whimsical ice cream candles look so yummy that you may be almost tempted to eat them. They are perfect accents for a child's party and will be remembered long after all the real food is finished!

Making these candles requires patience and a thorough understanding of all the techniques discussed earlier in this book. The analogy between candle making and the culinary arts is obvious in this project, whose end result looks like the real thing!

As it cools, liquid wax can be whipped in much the same way as you beat egg whites to make a meringue. Once whipped, the wax can be sculpted into gravity-defying shapes, and as it cools it will harden and set. You may find that when you have mastered ice cream candles, you will find yourself dreaming up other wax culinary delights you can create.

If you dye the wax before whipping it, you can create the look of different flavors of ice cream. You can mold it in tins to create wax cakes, pies, breads, cookies, and biscuits. You can also mold it in a glass to resemble beer or ale.

The wax must be whipped vigorously, and it may be difficult to prevent splashing. Make sure that your work area is well protected, and wear an apron to protect your clothes.

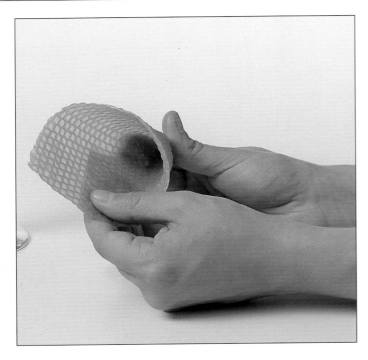

Roll the beeswax triangle into a cone and press the outside free end in place.

Melt the undyed wax in the double boiler and remove it from the heat. As the wax cools, a skin starts to form on the surface. At this point, start to whip the wax with the fork.

As you continue whipping, air is beaten into the wax, which cools it rapidly. Keep whipping until the wax starts to stiffen; then, using the ice cream scoop, quickly spoon the wax into the cone and shape it. If the frothy wax is too hot when you scoop it, it will soften and become misshapen. If it is too cold, it will harden and become unworkable.

For extra flavor, melt a little red wax in the small pan and trickle the hot red syrup over the ice cream. Heat the wicking needle, then poke it into the center of the ice cream and down into the cone. Pull out the needle and quickly insert the wick into the hole. You can top off the ice cream with a real red raspberry and a tiny umbrella to pretty it up and add to its authenticity.

Materials and equipment
Triangular piece of natural beeswax, with 6" sides
3 1/2 oz. of undyed white wax
Small amount of red wax (optional)
Primed wick
Double boiler
Fork or hand beater
Ice cream scoop
Small pan
Wicking needle

Skill level: Advanced

Calla lily candles

Materials and equipment
Clear undyed wax mixed with
10 percent stearin
Yellow and green wax dyes
Primed wick, 6" long
Small pan
Double boiler
Metal pie pan
Thermometer
Crafts knife
Freezer paper
Skewer, chopstick, or dowel
Wicking needle

Skill level: Advanced

The dramatic lines and translucent delicacy of these strikingly elegant wax flowers makes them a perennial favorite. Making these calla lily candles involves several techniques discussed earlier in this book. The trickiest part of making the candle is judging the proper time to cut and shape the wax for the petal. The shape will be very delicate before the wax has set. Afterward, the candles are surprisingly sturdy.

Put enough wax and yellow dye in the small pan so that, when melted, the wax will be at least 5" deep. Heat the wax to 15°F and use it to make a short yellow taper 3/8" in diameter to be the pistil of the flower.

Heat clear undyed wax in the double boiler. Make sure the pie pan is perfectly flat and level, then pour wax into the pan to a depth of 1/8".

Allow the wax to cool until it becomes white and opaque but still warm and pliable. Using the crafts knife, quickly cut an oval in the wax and lift it

out of the pan. Gently curl the edges of the oval to form the conical shape of the petal.

Carefully hold the petal in your hand until the wax has set enough so that it won't become misshapen, then carefully place it on the freezer paper to completely harden.

Trim and taper the base of the yellow pistil until it test-fits snugly into the base of the white petal. Dip the base of the pistil into 176°F yellow wax for 2 seconds,

then slip the pistil quickly into the petal. Set the flower aside to cool and harden.

Add the green dye to clear wax in the double boiler and heat it to 158°F. Overdip the base of the flower in the green dye for 2 seconds, then remove and allow to cool. Repeat 3 more times.

Warm the wicking needle and carefully press it into the base of the flower to make a hole for inserting the skewer or dowel that will be the stem.

Carefully insert the stem into the hole and with your fingers mold the warm wax at the base of the flower around the stem. Set aside to cool and harden. If the joining of the flower and stem doesn't seem secure, you can make a small leaf with green wax in the same manner you made the petal; curl and bold the leaf around the flower base and stem.

After you have mastered making one calla lily, you might want to make a whole bouquet. You can also adapt the techniques given here to make a wide variety of different flowers.

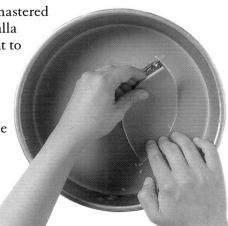

DECORATED
CANDLES

You can make your own candles to decorate or purchase
them. There are so many ways of decorating a candle
that the only limit is your creativity. In this section of
the book, neither the techniques nor the ideas are
definitive, but they are presented to spark your
imagination.

Gold candles

These golden candles give a richness and opulence to any classical decorative theme. The best material for painting a candle is hot dyed wax, as this is naturally the most compatible colorant with the surface of the candle, but you can also use a golden spray paint as well as oil-based and acrylic paints.

> *Materials and equipment*
>
> *White pillar candle*
> *Rubber gloves*
> *Gold spray paint*
>
> *Skill level: Intermediate*

Before any candle is painted, it should be wiped with a lint-free cloth dampened slightly with alcohol, to remove any oils. Be careful to avoid getting paint onto the wick, which might hamper proper burning.

When using spray paint, always follow the manufacturer's directions and apply the spray in a well-ventilated area.

Wearing rubber gloves, grasp the wick of the candle between your thumb and forefinger. Carefully spray a very thin coat of paint over the entire candle. Set aside for a few minutes to allow the paint to dry, then repeat. Build up the depth of the paint with several light coats rather than one thick one, to prevent unsightly runs and drips.

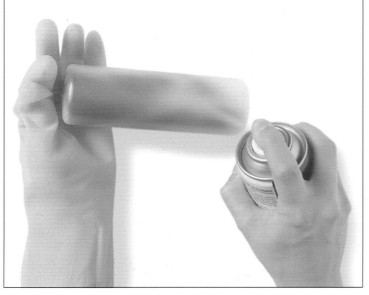

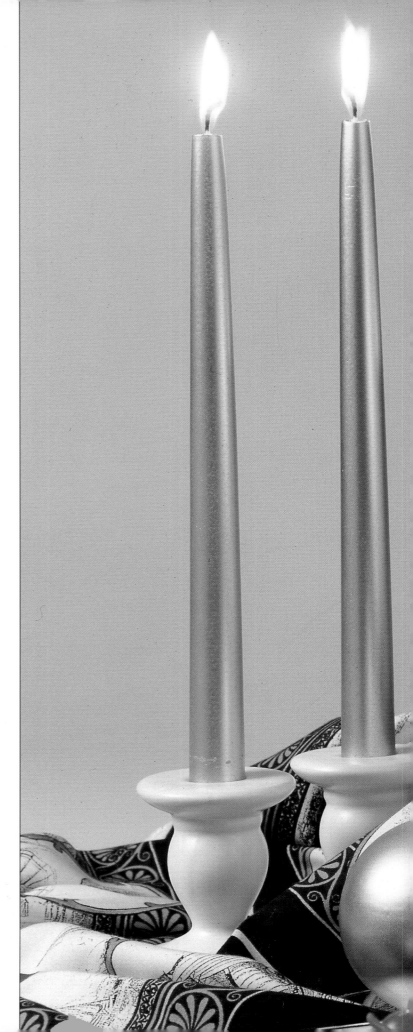

Hand-painted candles

Painted designs on ordinary household and pillar candles can be as simple or as extravagant as you wish. Painting is a simple way to dress up plain-Jane candles.

It's an ideal way of decorating them to fit a particular season, holiday, occasion, or theme.

The best material for painting candles is hot dyed wax. Oil-based paint can also be used, but the easiest method is to use water-based acrylic paints mixed with a few drops of dish detergent, which creates a smooth mixture that is easy to apply, quick to dry, and adheres well to the candle.

Hold the candle at the base, and work around the candle from top to bottom to avoid smudging areas you have already painted. You could paint a regular all-over design such as blue stars or some free-form multicolor flowers.

When you have finished the painting, place the candle into a candlestick and allow it to thoroughly dry before handling. To protect the painted design, overdip the candle very quickly in wax heated to 203°F. This will glaze the design onto the candle.

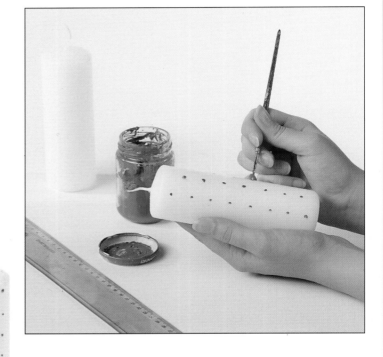

Materials and equipment
White pillar candle
Paints
Small paintbrushes

Skill level: Beginner

Stenciled candles

Stenciling has in recent years become a widely popular decorating technique. It is an effective method of decorating candles. Stencils are particularly useful for making repeat patterns.

M easure the circumference and height of the candle, then cut a piece of stencil paper to those dimensions. Draw your design on the paper. Cut out the design with the crafts knife.

S pray the back of the stencil with spray adhesive and tightly wrap it around the candle. It is a good idea to use masking tape to seal the seam where the edges meet.

U se the stencil brush to apply the paint, being careful not to get paint on the wick. When the paint is dry, carefully remove the stencil.

A n alternative to cutting a stencil is to use a paper doily that has delicate filigree patterns cut out of it. Patterned lace trim found in fabric or notions shops will give a similar effect.

Stamped candles

Materials and equipment

Candle
Acrylic paint
Rubber stamp
Stencil brush

Skill level: Intermediate

Another decorating technique that is very popular for repeat patterns on candles is stamping.

You can purchase stamps in an infinite variety of designs or make your own.

Carefully apply a thin layer of paint to the stamp by lightly tapping the paint onto the stamp with the stencil brush.

Stamp the surface of the candle. To stamp on curved surfaces, apply one edge of the stamp to the surface of the candle and firmly but carefully roll the stamp around the candle and lift it off.

If wet paint gets smudged, it can be wiped away with a damp cloth.

Cut and curled candles

Materials and equipment

*Rainbow dipped candle
(preferably freshly dipped and
still slightly warm)
Hair dryer
Crafts knife*

Skill level: Intermediate

Cut and curled dipped candles have a unique feathery appearance that compliments contemporary styles and more rustic country settings. This technique can be difficult to master, but with practice and patience, you will be a pro in no time.

You will find that by overdipping triangular, rectangular, and star-shape candles in different colors and cutting and curling the corners, it is possible to create some incredibly exotic candles.

Place the hair dryer on your work surface so that warm air from it constantly blows on the candle as you work. Keeping the candle warm is essential for successful curling.

Hold the base of the candle in one hand, and with the crafts knife make a shallow slanting cut, starting at the top of the candle and cutting diagonally about 3/4" down toward the base of the candle and slightly in toward the wick.

With your thumb against the cut surface of the candle, carefully slip the knife up and out of the cut, curling the wax outward and away from the wick. Make sure you keep the candle warm, and be careful not to break the curl.

Rotate the candle 180° and make a second curl opposite the first one.

Make a second pair of curls about 3/4" below the first pair, then make a third pair between the second pair so that there are 4 equidistant curls on the second tier.

Continue working downward to cut 4-curl tiers until you reach the base of the candle.

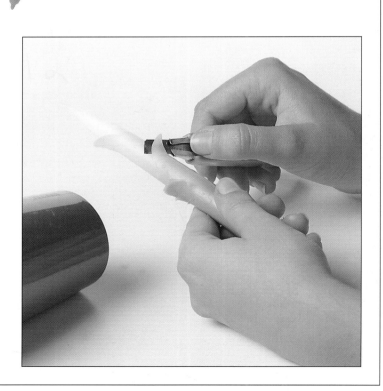

Carved candles

Materials and equipment

White pillar candle
Blue wax
Small V-shape leather or
linoleum carving tool
Stiff-bristled brush

Skill level: Intermediate

Carved candles have a wonderful three-dimensional quality, especially when they are lit and the candle flame glows through the carving. This simple but effective technique gives the candles a warm, hand-made feel.

The carving itself is relatively straightforward, but the candles need to be specially prepared for this project. They should be round and smooth, (ball and pillar candles are ideal), and they must be white.

To prepare the candles for carving, overdip them 2 or 3 times in blue wax at 165°F. The color of the wax must be deep and intense, so use at least twice the ordinary amount of dye to mix up the blue wax. After overdipping, the coating of the candle should be a richly colored but very thin layer.

The secret of successful carving is to make each cut in two separate passes. Make the first cut very gently into the outer colored surface, then carve again, more deeply, to reveal the inner white wax. If the first cut is too deep, it may chip and break the blue layer.

With the carving tool, cut a shallow straight or curved line from the top of the candle to the bottom. (Straight lines are easier to carve than curved lines.) Carve again to reveal the white wax underneath.

Brush away any loose wax with the stiff brush.

Starting at the top of the long carved line on the candle a small distance from the line and working inward to it, carve small lines to resemble caterpillar legs. Repeat down the entire length of the long line, on both sides of it, then brush away any loose wax.

Shaker candles

Materials and equipment

Pure paraffin wax (no stearin)
Wax dyes, red and green
White pillar candle
2 cookie sheets
Thermometer
Cookie cutter, star shape
Rotary cutter
Pot of boiling water
Slender spatula
Hair dryer

Skill level: Intermediate

This Shaker candle was inspired by a style of early American furnishings. As the candle slowly burns, its light glows through the wax shapes that decorate it, like a ray of sunlight through stained glass.

Dye and heat a batch of green wax to 194°F. Pour the melted wax onto a cookie sheet to a depth of 1/8". Repeat for red wax, using the second cookie sheet. Allow the wax to cool until slightly firm but still malleable. Heat the base of the pillar candle with the hair dryer.

Using the cookie cutter, cut small shapes from the sheet of red wax. Heat the spatula in the boiling water, wipe it off, and then use it to release the shapes from the cookie sheet. Position the spatula against the candle, slide out the spatula, and press the shape in place.

Using the crafts knife, cut several strips of soft-set green wax and remove them from the cookie sheet. Wrap the strips around the top, bottom, and middle of the pillar candle as shown or as desired.

Allow the candle to completely cool and harden.

Mosaic-tile candles

Materials and equipment

White pyramid candle
Wax dye, 3 different colors
3 cookie sheets
Crafts knife
*Hair dryer, hot spatula,
or wax glue*

Skill level: Beginner

These pyramid candles are decorated with colored mosaic tiles cut from wax sheets.

The techniques used to make a tiled candle are very similar to those used to make the Shaker candle. Both types of candles have colored wax shapes applied with heat or wax glue. The more colors used, the better. Candles with straight, not curved, sides work best for tiling.

Dye and heat 3 different colors of wax to 194°F and pour them onto individual cookie sheets to a thickness of 1/8". Allow to cool and harden. Detach the sheets of wax from the cookie sheets and, using the crafts knife, cut shapes approximately 3/8" square. To stick them to the candle, either heat the surface of the candle with a hot spatula or use wax glue.

To give the candle a smooth, glossy finish, dip it for a second or two in 194°F melted wax. Allow to cool completely.

Candles for keeping time

Materials and equipment

A box of commercially manufactured white household, pillar, or tapered candles
Masking tape
Ruler
Pencil
Paints and paintbrushes

Skill level: Intermediate

Before the invention of the mechanical clock, the time keeping candle was very common in churches and convents, and it would tell people when it was prayer time. Making an accurate time keeping candle is relatively simple, once you have figured out how much a candle burns down in a given burn time, usually one hour.

To determine how far your candles will burn in an hour, you first measure the length of a test candle and then light it. Blow out the test candle once an hour has passed and measure the candle again. Subtract the second measurement from the first to determine the distance burned down in one hour (If the top of your candle is tapered, you may want to measure after 1 hour and again after 2 hours. The distance burned down during the second hour is the distance you'll use as your basic unit.)

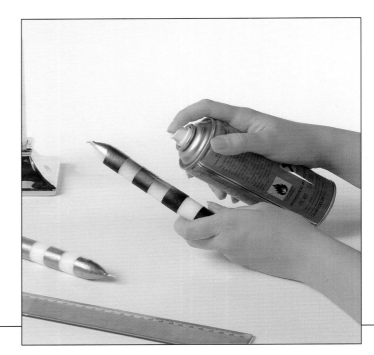

Prepare the candle you wish to paint by cleaning it with a soft cloth moistened with alcohol.

Using the pencil and ruler, mark the hour distances on the candle, starting at the bottom and working upward toward the top. The number of marks is the total number of hours that your candle will burn.

Starting at either the top or bottom of the candle, cover alternate spaces between pencil marks with masking tape, winding it completely around the candle. Paint the unprotected areas of the candle. Allow the paint to dry. Remove the tape.

Outdoor torches

Materials and equipment

Paraffin wax mixed with 10% stearin
Wax dye
Old cotton shirt cut into 3"-wide strips
Bamboo poles 36" long (available at gardening centers)
Double boiler
Thermometer
Rubber gloves
Sturdy wire

Skill level: Beginner

The sun sets over the sea and in our garden or on the terrace, the party lights come on. Outdoor torches (also known as beach torches) have always been favorite accessories for summer parties because of the large amount of light they provide. Once the torches are anchored in the sand, be sure to keep adults and children alike away from them. Observe all fire safety precautions.

These torches produce a long-lasting flame. To extinguish one, cover the flame with dry sand and wait until the torch has completely cooled before touching it.

Wrap a 6" length of wire tightly around the wick to secure it to the pole.

Pour the rest of the hot wax into the dipping can, then briefly dip the entire wick into the wax.

Make the torches outside over ground covered with newspapers.

Dye and melt the wax in the double boiler and bring the temperature to 194°F. Wearing the rubber gloves, soak a strip of shirting cotton into the hot wax, holding one end between your fingers. When it is well soaked in scalding wax, lay the fabric on the bamboo pole, then wrap the strip tightly around the end of the stick. Allow to cool for a few minutes.

Repeat with additional wax-soaked strips of cotton until the cotton wick on the stick measures 1 1/2" thick.

Candle shades

Construction paper makes quick and easy
candle shades.

Step-by-step

Materials and equipment

Construction paper
Ruler, pencil, and compass
Scissors
Glue
2 paper clips or clamps
Decorating materials

Skill level: Intermediate

This shade is made from colored construction paper. It is shaped like a cone and has a 2"-wide top opening.

U se the ruler to draw a line 12" wide on your construction paper. Use the compass to draw two concentric semicircles above the line, one 2" and one 6" in radius. Mark off a 30-degree wedge at one end of the semicircles.

U se the scissors to cut along the semicircles; discard the wedge.

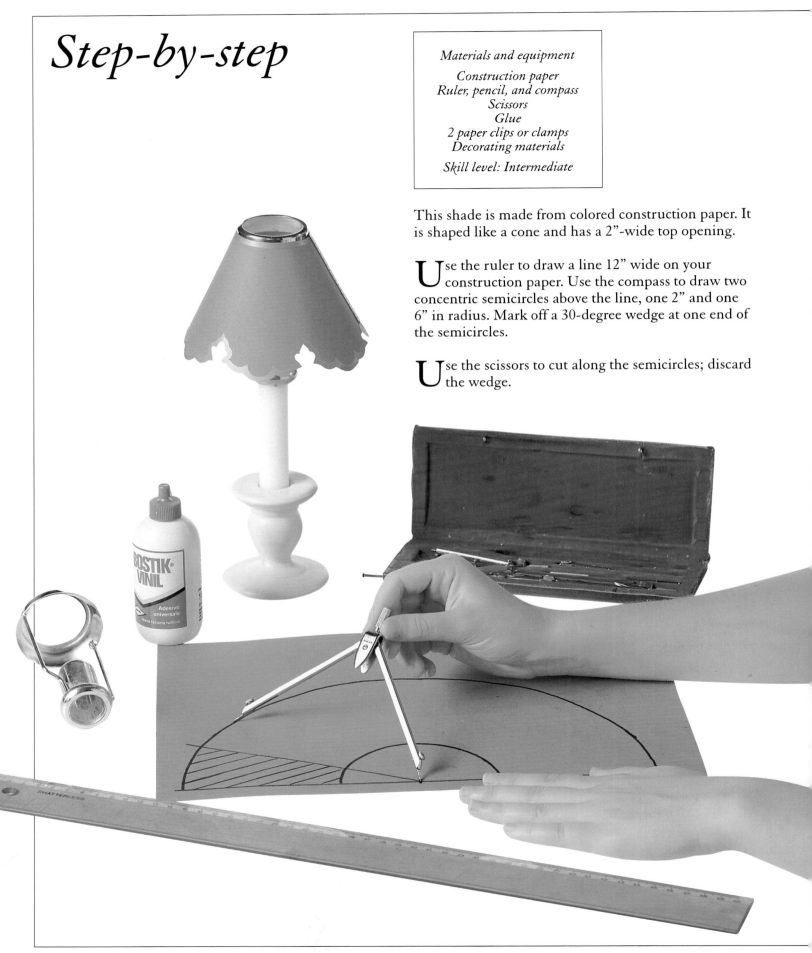

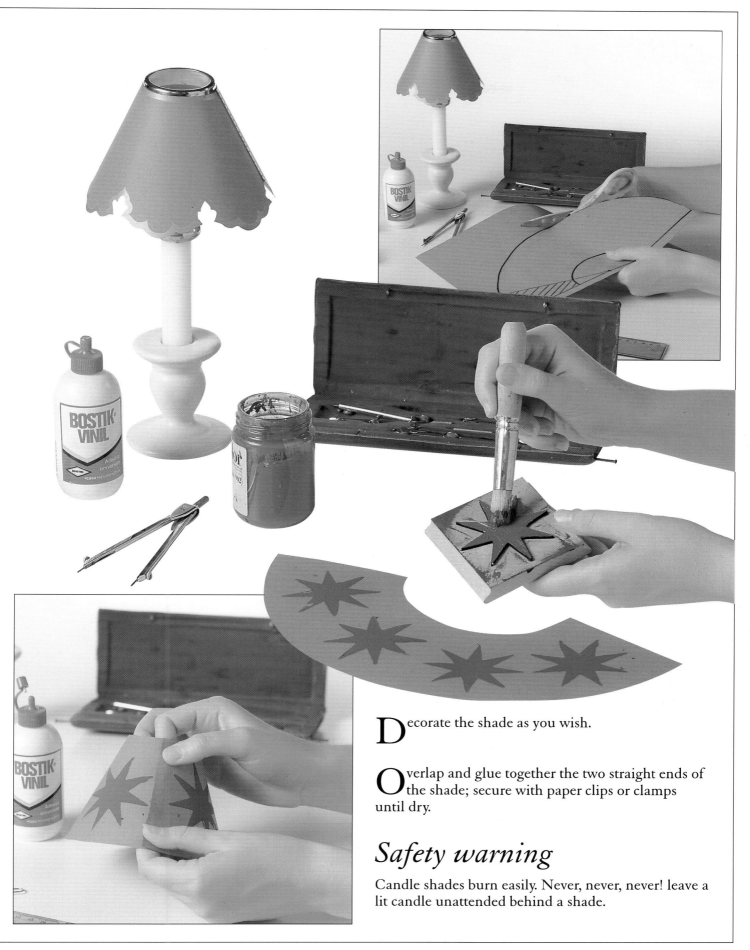

D ecorate the shade as you wish.

O verlap and glue together the two straight ends of the shade; secure with paper clips or clamps until dry.

Safety warning

Candle shades burn easily. Never, never, never! leave a lit candle unattended behind a shade.

ARTISTIC CANDLES

M.U.M. candles

The I Ceri shop in Milan, Italy, stocks unusual handmade candles from Turkey. If these candles remind you of ancient times, maybe it is because their bold architectural features were inspired by archaeological discoveries. Some of the candles are very large and have multiple wicks. Because of their size, they work well in large, spacious rooms or among classic furniture and decor.

Graziani candles

Graziani is one of the oldest Italian candle factories. Founded in 1805 by Abramo Graziani, the business is run today, six generations later, by his great-great-great-grandson Mario.
The Graziani wax factory was the first to introduce candle making in molds, more than 150 years ago. Many of its original molds are pillar and ball molds that are still in use today.
Graziani also makes candles used by many churches.

Millefiori candles

These beautiful handmade candles are
reminiscent of Millefiori Venetian glass.
They are made with wax of the highest quality
and special coloring agents that give them their
distinctive bright colors.
When a Millefiori candle is lit, and the flame
gleams through the colors and illuminates them,
the overall effect is truly magical!

Point à la Ligne

Point à la Ligne is a French company that specializes in making designer candles that are known around the world.
The flower-shaped candles are particularly striking and popular.
Visiting the shop or even browsing through a catalog can be very inspirational to home candle makers.

Inès de la Fressange

Inès de la Fressange is a French fashion designer who also designs many of the extravagant candles manufactured by Point à la Ligne. She uses soft colors that give her creations a very special charm that works with any decor.

Afterword

As this book shows, candle making is a bit like cooking. A few basic ingredients, techniques, timing, and temperature combine to produce a menu of endless variety for all occasions.

Candle making is a fascinating craft that can be enjoyed by the whole family. After you have mastered the basic skills, you can start creating your own candle recipes.

There are many suppliers of candle making equipment. Most crafts stores stock it. But if you have trouble finding what you need, you can usually substitute common household items successfully.

Yogurt cups and other household items can be used as molds. If you have trouble finding wax with stearin already added, you can buy cheap boxes of household candles and melt them down. As a bonus you also get primed wicks! Instead of commercial wax dyes to give you exactly the color wax you want, you can substitute wax crayons as long as they are pure wax.

Remember:
A correctly made candle will burn evenly with a clean flame and no smoke. There will be no excess melted wax to drip or for the wick to drown in.
A candle must set for at least 24 hours before being lit.
Do not play with lit candles. Not only can this create a fire hazard, but it may also interfere with the way the candle burns.
Keep wicks trimmed to about 1/2" long.
Never burn candles in a draft.

Troubleshooting

If a finished candle does not burn correctly, you can usually track down the cause. The following chart lists some of the most common symptoms, their probable causes, and best solutions.

SYMPTOM	CAUSE	SOLUTION
Dripping	Draft	Move candle out of the draft
Wax too soft	Incorrect wax/stearin mix	Mix a new batch
Candle will not burn	Unprimed wick	Invert candle and light it
Damp wick	Various	Place candle somewhere warm and dry for 48 hours
Small flame	Wax too hard	Check wax/stearin mix
Flame too small	Wick was cut too short	Use a longer wick, or cut away wax from around the wick
Smoking candle	Wick too long	Trim wick, or use a shorter wick
Drowned wick	Wick too short	Use a longer wick, or cut wax away from around the wick
Loose wick	Tension too loose when wicked up	Increase tension of wick when wicking up
Sputtering flame	Damp wick	Place candle somewhere warm and dry for 48 hours

Dipped candles

The following charts list symptoms, causes, and solutions for some of the more common problems encountered when making candles that are dipped or molded.

Symptom	Cause	Solution
Lumpy surface	First dip was too fast, or wax was too cold.	Warm the candle and roll it on a smooth surface. Overdip in wax at 194°F for 2 seconds.
White marks on candle surface	Wax too cold	Overdip in wax at 203°F for 2 seconds.
Candle cracks during rolling.	Uneven candle temperature (i.e., center is harder than outside)	Redip until candle softens.
Bent candle	Bent wick	Straighten the wick between dips as it cools.

Symptom	Cause	Solution
Air bubbles	Wax was poured too fast.	Pour wax more slowly.
	Mold was not tapped.	Tap sides of mold after pouring wax to remove air bubbles.
Wax cools too fast	Wax not hot enough	
Spaces have formed between candle and mold	Wax shrank during setting.	Add more hot wax to fill the spaces that have formed. When taking the candle out of the mold, wax indents or outdents appear. Use a crafts knife to trim the candle, then dip it in 203°F hot wax for 2 seconds.
Different colored waxes blend together	The set wax wasn't hard enough when a subsequent layer was poured.	Use the candle as it is, or melt it and begin again.
One layer of colored wax doesn't blend with its neighboring color.	Layers of different color wax are melted at different temperatures.	Melt the wax and use it again.
The candle cannot be taken out of the mold.	Not enough stearin	Heat the mold, using the hair dryer.
The wax thickens too slowly.		Put the candle in the refrigerator.
Wax oozes out the opening of the mold.	Care was not taken when positioning the wick.	Put the base of the mold immediately under cold water and clog the hole with mold sealer.
Stains or fading in the color of the wax	Impurities in the wax or coloring	Always keep your tools and molds clean.

Glossary

BURNING POINT
The point of the candle where the wick protrudes from it for burning.

CARVING
The process of decoratively cutting into candles, usually with a carving tool.

CLEAR WAX
Paraffin wax with no added stearin or dyes.

COOLING
The process of allowing or causing wax or candles to decrease in temperature.

CORE CANDLE
A small candle used as a foundation on which to build a larger candle.

CUTTING
A technique for altering the shape of a candle without actually removing any wax.

DIPPING
The process of immersing a wick or candle in molten wax.

DIPPING CAN
Tall cylindrical pot specifically used for dipping.

DRYING
The process of allowing candles to cool and completely solidify. Drying takes at least one hour.

DYE
Pigment used for coloring wax.

DYEING
The process of adding color pigment to wax.

HOURLY BURN
The length of a candle that will burn down in one hour.

HOUSEHOLD CANDLE
Short white pillar candle, about 3/4" x 7 1/2".

MOLD
Container into which hot wax is poured to create a shaped candle.

MOLDING
The process of forming wax into a specific shape.

MOLD SEALER
A puttylike compound specifically intended to seal molds in order to make them waterproof.

RELEASE AGENT
A slick compound (such as salad oil or petroleum jelly) used to facilitate the removal of candles from molds.

STEARIN
A chemical additive for wax that causes it to harden and shrink.

TAPER
A thin candle, wider at the base than the top.

WAX
Paraffin wax, unless otherwise specified.

WAX GLUE
A special glue designed for sticking wax to itself or other materials.

WICK
A braided cotton cord designed to absorb molten wax and deliver it to the burning point.

Lighting and extinguishing candles

LIGHTING

Before lighting a candle, make sure the length of the wick is correct; it should measure 3/8"-1/2". If the candle is new, you may have to shorten the wick to the right length and then free a section from the wax covering it.

The best way of lighting a candle is with another candle. Making a lighting candle is simple: Dip and redip a wick in melted wax until the taper reaches 1/8"-3/16" in diameter.

If you prefer, you can also use a match, lighter, or fire starter to light a candle.

EXTINGUISHING

It is common practice to blow on a candle to extinguish it, which tends to bend the wick and drown it in molten wax.

The best way to extinguish a flame is to deprive it of oxygen. A candle snuffer is the ideal tool, but there are other items that can also act as a snuffer. If you don't have one, you can wet your thumb and forefinger and use them to pinch out the flame on the wick.

In the past, when candle lighting was an important part of everyday life, knowing how to light and extinguish one properly were seen as very important skills. You can turn them into modern-day rituals if you like and pass them down to future generations.

Index

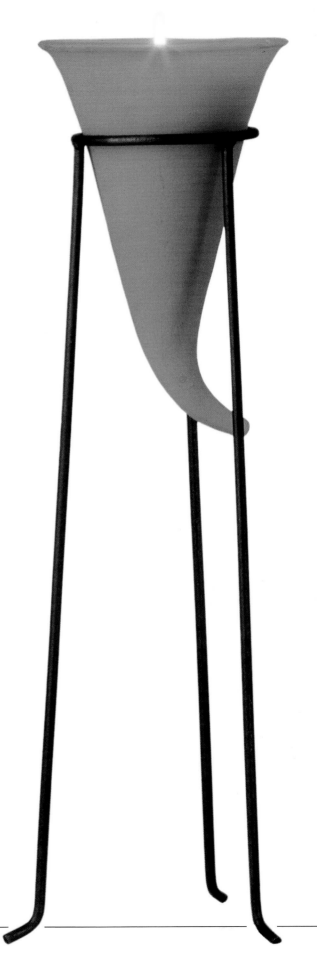